Friend Grief and The Military:

BAND OF FRIENDS

VICTORIA NOE

Copyright © 2014 by Victoria Noe

Cover design: Rebecca Swift

Editor: Melissa Wuske

All rights reserved. This book or any portion thereof may not be reproduced or used in any manner whatsoever without the express written permission of the publisher except for the use of brief quotations in a book review.

This book is not intended as a substitute for therapeutic or medical advice. The reader should regularly consult a medical professional in matters relating to his/her health and particularly with respect to any symptoms that may require diagnosis or medical attention.

For a list of grief support resources: FriendGrief.com

Printed in the United States of America

First Printing, 2014

ISBN   978-0-9903081-0-2 (paperback)
           978-0-9903081-1-9 (epub)
           978-0-9903081-2-6 (mobi)

King Company – Chicago, IL 60618

Permissions

"Empty Chairs at Empty Table", from the musical *Les Misérables*. Music by: Claude-Michel Schönberg Lyrics by: Alain Boublil and Herbert Kretzmer © Alain Boublil Music Ltd.

Sister in the Band of Brothers: Embedded with the 101st Airborne in Iraq, by Katherine M. Skiba, published by the University Press of Kansas © 2005. www.kansaspress.ku.edu. Used by permission of the publisher.

Excerpt from *Soldier From The War Returning* by Thomas Childers. Copyright ©2009 by Thomas Childers. Used by permission of Houghton Mifflin Harcourt Publishing Company. All rights reserved.

From *They Fought For Each Other: The Triumph and Tragedy of the Hardest Hit Unit in Iraq* by Kelly Kennedy. Reprinted by permission of St. Martin's Press. All rights reserved.

From *On Call in Hell: A Doctor's Iraq War Story* by Richard Jadick, with Thomas Hayden, copyright ©2007 by Richard Jadick. Used by permission of Dutton Signet, a division of Penguin

"PTSD vs. Moral Injury" (Venn diagram) from *Moral Injury: The Grunts,* Huffington Post, March 8, 2014.

Table of Contents

Dedication vii

Introduction 1

Friend or Brother? 5

Watching Your Friends Die 7

Delayed Grief 11

Non-combatants 15

Chaplains 21

"Through the Gates of Hell for a Wounded Marine" 27

Embedded 35

"Never Shall I Fail My Comrades"– Guilt 43

PTSD and Moral Injury 47

Suicide 55

Resilience 61

Acknowledgements 69

References: 71

Resources: 75

Dedication

Oh my friends, my friends forgive me.

That I live and you are gone

There's a grief that can't be spoken

There's a pain goes on and on.

"Empty Chairs at Empty Table"

Introduction

Let's begin with what this book is not:

It's not about stereotypical "crazy" veterans, a generality especially associated with those who fought in Vietnam.

It's not about the inevitability of suicide among our active duty military and veterans.

It's not about condemning those who served in recent wars as less able to withstand the rigors of combat than those who fought in previous conflicts.

It's not an indictment of the training or suitability of troops – in the US or in other countries.

It's not even an opinion on the morality or politics of war.

Instead, it's an attempt to put the unique bond between battle buddies in perspective: to show that the friendships forged in the heat of war are unique and life-changing.

It's an attempt to show that the strength of those friendships cannot be over-estimated, because they are friendships constantly threatened with death.

It's an attempt to show that the grief experienced when those friends die – in battle or from suicide – is unlike the grief experienced by civilians.

It's a grief that deserves as much respect as a chest full of medals.

And finally, it's an attempt to show the resilience of these brave men and women – those on the battlefield and those who support them in the field – including their fierce determination to ensure that their fallen comrades are not forgotten.

What exactly, then, *is* this kind of grief?

Everyone experiences grief at some time, and that grief is often for a friend. What makes the grief experienced by men and women in the military unique are two factors:

First, their grief fits the definition of "complicated" grief, which refers to the factors that separate it from the "normal' experience of grieving a loved one.

Consider this list from the 2012 US Marine Corps *Leaders Guide for Managing Marines in Distress:*

Types of losses that can lead to complicated grief:

- The death of a close friend, such as a 'battle buddy'
- The death of a valued leader or mentor
- The death of someone with whom the Marine closely identified
- The death of someone for whom the Marine felt personally responsible
- A death that is believed to have been preventable
- A particularly violent or gruesome death

By this definition, then, complicated grief is the norm in the military. It would not be surprising for someone to face all of these losses *at the same time*. This is not the grief for a friend who died peacefully in their sleep at the age of 90. This is the grief for a 20 year old who was blown to bits before your eyes. So when I refer to grief in this book, this definition is what I'm referencing.

Second, having experienced this, there is often little chance of grieving normally. *The Guide* goes on to discourage immediate psychological debriefing for a unit that has experienced the loss of a member or members. Instead, the leaders are encouraged to:

- Get the unit to safety as soon as possible
- Rest the unit for 24-72 hours, if at all possible
- Encourage discussions in squad-sized After-Action Reviews of what happened, why it happened, what will be done to prevent it from happening again (if possible), and what purpose was served by the sacrifice
- Reinforce the rules of engagement and Law of War, and remind your Marines that revenge not only dishonors the Corps and those who have sacrificed, but it also is self-defeating in a counterinsurgency conflict
- Honor the fallen through memorial services, physical memorials, and other celebrations

Perhaps you noticed, as I did, how often the word "possible" is used: "as soon as possible", "if possible", "if at all possible". Grief is typically put on hold, because to acknowledge it – let alone express it – requires calling a time-out.

That's not always possible in the midst of battle. But grieving is necessary, as John McCary insisted in a letter from Iraq to his mother in 2004:

> When you've held a conversation with a man, briefed him on his mission, his objective, and reminded him of the potential consequences during the actioning of it, only to hear he never returned, and did not die gracefully, though blessedly quickly, prayerfully painlessly…you do not breathe the same ever after. Breath is sweet. Sleep is sweeter. Friends are priceless. And you cry. There's no point, no gain, no benefit but you are human and you must mourn. It is your nature.

Think about the times you've grieved the death of a friend. Go back to the list of factors leading to complicated grief. Now you'll begin to understand that what we're going to consider here is something very, very different.

Friend or Brother?

The popular mini-series *Band of Brothers* took its title from what has become known as the St. Crispan's Day speech in Shakespeare's *Henry V*:

> This story shall the good man teach his son;
>
> And Crispin Crispian shall ne'er go by,
>
> From this day to the ending of the world,
>
> But we in it shall be remembered –
>
> We few, we happy few, we band of brothers;
>
> For he to-day that sheds his blood with me
>
> Shall be my brother…

Since Shakespeare's time we've often heard soldiers, sailors and Marines refer to their battle buddies as "brothers".

Even though it's somewhat problematic, given the increasing role of women on the front lines, the designation has stuck.

In writings as far back as the ancient Greeks, the relationship between soldiers has been described as comparable to family. A family is a group of people related by blood that functions together with common goals and dependency. "Blood is thicker than water," right?

In the military, nothing can be accomplished without the trust and dependability of those in the unit. That cohesiveness is the difference between success and failure, life and death, every hour of every day. The bond is stronger than a normal friendship because your lives depend on it. So, when asked why they refer to their friends as brothers, you are likely to get an answer along the lines of "because they mean as much to me as family." Referring to other soldiers as family members is, from their perspective, the highest compliment.

A similar phenomenon existed in the AIDS community in the 80s and 90s. People with HIV/AIDS – gay, straight, young, old, male, female – were often abandoned by their families. Their friends became their family of choice – of necessity, really – because their lives depended on them.

Conventional wisdom still holds that the bond between family members is normally stronger than that between friends. But I wonder why, considering this quote that's quite a bit older than Shakespeare's:

"Greater love has no one than this: to lay down one's life for one's friends." (John 15:13)

That's why this book is not titled *Band of Brothers* or *Band of Brothers and Sisters*.

This book is titled *Band of Friends*.

Watching Your Friends Die

They were killing my friends.

That was the reason given by Audie Murphy, one of the most decorated American soldiers in World War II, when he was awarded the Congressional Medal of Honor for taking on an entire German company single-handed. Not the mission, not the politics – just the fact the enemy was killing his friends.

Civilians are lucky. Unless we're first responders or work in a hospital it's rare that we witness anyone's death. We may even hope to be with someone – family member or close friend – when they die. We don't want them to be frightened, alone, far away, or – worst of all – in pain.

But imagine what it must be like: your friends dying horrific deaths, sometimes in front of you. The randomness is often the most disturbing, in this description from Thomas Childers' *Soldier From the War Returning: The Greatest Generation's Troubled Homecoming from World War II*, about a veteran of that war:

> For two years, he had lived in a world where death was a daily occurrence, a pitiless, irrevocable fact. Men disappeared or came back splattered across the turrets or cockpit or radio compartment. They were at chow in the morning, and then they were gone – empty bunks at the barracks, their personal effects sorted and sent home to grieving families. He had lost buddies and watched helplessly as day after day men failed to return from their missions. At Air Station 153, they did not dwell on these things. They could not. Eventually, he had come to accept the war's brutal, inexplicable realities, its immutable cruelty. He had stopped looking for explanations. The men endured it; they moved on.

Troops around the world are well-trained for going to war. Even in the adrenaline surge before a battle, they know intellectually that they or their friends could die. But as others in this book will tell you, nothing can truly prepare you for what you're going to experience.

Today, as one soldier put it, "a dead cat is not always a dead cat": just because something looks benign, doesn't mean it might not actually be a disguised IED (Improvised Explosive Device). If someone picks it up, or kicks it aside, it could trigger an explosion large enough to engulf a Humvee in flames. Air strikes are called in from far away. Women and children may be used as shields, or they may be the ones shooting at you from their homes. The enemy is everywhere: in the streets, in caves or in schools. And they can hide effectively. If you leave the bodies of your comrades behind, they might not only be picked over for valuables: you can count on them being desecrated.

David Finkel, in his 2013 book *Thank You For Your Service*, gives as good a description as you will ever read of the overwhelming, relentless loss of life witnessed by soldiers in the field:

> They had seen Harrelson's Humvee rise into the air and burst into fire. They had seen Emory get shot in the head and collapse in his own spreading blood…They had heard a doctor say, "I'm hoping, I'm hoping," about a soldier who in a few minutes would be dead. They had heard a soldier tell a dying soldier as he stuffed what was left of him into a Humvee, "You're gonna have to move your feet so I can close the door."…They had heard a sergeant who was watching something skid across the floor of the aid station, which had fallen from a shredded soldier who was about to die, say with sadness, "That's a toe." They had heard Aieti ask in the most hopeful voice a soldier could ever muster, "What happened to Harrelson?"

Delayed Grief

Pushing aside your own needs for a greater cause seems heroic, but most veterans reject the idea that they are heroes. They insist that they were doing what they had to do: to complete their mission, to stay alive, to protect their comrades who were still alive. They had to focus on the present, pushing down their grief and the horror of what they witnessed until a time somewhere in the future. They did not have the luxury to grieve when it happened.

Thousands of books have been written on how to grieve. While all approach it from the belief that everyone grieves in their own way, there are some truths that are held to be universal. Perhaps the most important one is to accept your grief. Don't push it away. Don't ignore it. Don't deny yourself the need to grieve.

But how do you grieve when your friends are killed on the battlefield? And how does it affect you when you have no choice but to push that grief aside because the war continues?

Army Times writer Kelly Kennedy, embedded with Charlie Company 1-26, observed the company after one particularly devastating loss:

> Almost to a man, they guys had one similar response: They froze up, became numb. It wasn't necessarily intentional; it was more like their bodies and minds reacted in a way that allowed them to continue to try to survive. But it also kept them from dealing with their emotions. Consciously, as a group, they made a decision. If they thought about their lost friends, they thought about laughing and dancing and teasing – or else it was impossible to get back in the Humvee.

Those on the battlefield depend on their ability to focus on the task at hand, their capacity to put off that grief. The problem is that delayed grief is just that: delayed. Not gone, not resolved: delayed. It may retreat, but it always comes back. And as we'll see later in this book, when it does, the grieving does not come easily.

Perhaps no war monument, no battle anniversary, has evoked the demons of delayed grief like the Vietnam Memorial in Washington, DC. "The Wall", as it's known, was a controversial design: stark, black stone inscribed with the names of all those who died, in chronological order. No patriotic verses, no statues, no flags. Veterans and civilians alike considered the sight of 58,286 names depressing, disrespectful and disgraceful.

But it soon proved cathartic for the Vietnam veterans who visited: searching for names, making rubbings to take home, leaving dog tags, photos and other mementos of their time together. Volunteers – veterans themselves – staff a kiosk to direct visitors to specific names, but also to empathize and console. They know. They've been there.

Veterans are the only ones who truly understand what it was like to lose a friend in battle, as John McCary summarized on NPR and in *Operation Homecoming*:

> We have…so little time…to mourn, so little time to sigh, to breathe, to laugh, to remember. To forget. Every day awaits us, impatient, impending. So now we rise, shunning tears, biting back trembling lips and stifling sobs of grief…and we walk, shoulder to shoulder…to the Call of Duty, in tribute to the Fallen.

Civilians have the luxury – yes, the luxury – to grieve in their own time, at their own pace. They can take time off work when a friend dies to go to the wake or funeral. They send flowers or letters of condolence to their friend's family. They visit the cemetery. Normal grief, then, becomes another casualty of war.

Non-combatants

It's a broad category, non-combatants. For thousands of years there have been those at the battlefield who were not warriors: chaplains, doctors, nurses and medics as well as war correspondents. It could also include translators or civilian contractors. Regardless of job description, what they share is an inability to defend themselves in a dangerous and chaotic situation.

But non-combatants also share a special bond with the soldiers in the field – the men and women charged with keeping them safe – even while striving to remain professional, objective and focused in their jobs.

Most accounts of battles have focused on those who fought, but there are also those who never pick up a weapon. They may be civilians or medical personnel. They may be volunteers, eager to be part of the excitement. They may be men or women, or in the case of our little drummer boy, twelve years old.

Since non-combatants are rarely able to defend themselves when danger surrounds them, they depend on their unit to protect them. They are vulnerable, so when they die, those charged with their safety are doubly affected: by the loss of a friend and their perceived failure to save them.

One of the most famous non-combatants in literature was Rudyard Kipling's *Gunga Din*. The narrator is wounded in the field and is found by the water-carrier-who-wanted-to-be-a-soldier who has also been injured:

> 'E lifted up my 'ead,
>
> An' he plugged me where I bled,
>
> An' 'e guv me 'arf-a-pint o' water-green:
>
> It was crawlin' and it stunk,
>
> But of all the drinks I've drunk,
>
> I'm gratefullest to one from Gunga Din.
>
> > It was "Din! Din! Din!
>
> 'Ere's a beggar with a bullet through 'is spleen;
>
> 'E's chawin' up the ground,
>
> An' 'e's kickin' all around:
>
> For Gawd's sake git the water, Gunga Din!"
>
> 'E carried me away
>
> To where a dooli lay,
>
> An' a bullet come an' drilled the beggar clean.
>
> 'E put me safe inside,

An' just before 'e died,

"I 'ope you liked your drink", sez Gunga Din.

So I'll meet 'im later on

At the place where 'e is gone --

Where it's always double drill and no canteen.

'E'll be squattin' on the coals

Givin' drink to poor damned souls,

An' I'll get a swig in hell from Gunga Din!

    Yes, Din! Din! Din!

You Lazarushian-leather Gunga Din!

Though I've belted you and flayed you,

By the livin' Gawd that made you,

You're a better man than I am, Gunga Din.

Dr. L.P. Brockett, a prolific 19th century author, wrote a collection of "adventures of spies and scouts, daring exploits, heroic deeds, wonderful escapes, sanitary and hospital scenes, prison scenes, etc., etc., etc." in his 1866 book *The Camp, the Battlefield and the Hospital; or Lights and Shadows of the Great Rebellion*. In one of the quieter stories, "Night Scene in a Hospital", a nurse recounts when a young drummer boy was found sobbing after a nightmare:

> The boy came in with the rest, and the man who was taken dead from the ambulance was the Kit he mourned. Well he might; for, when the

wounded were brought from Fredericksburg, the child lay in one of the camps thereabout, and this good friend, though sorely hurt himself, would not leave him to the exposure and neglect of such a time and place; but, wrapping him in his own blanket, carried him in his arms to the transport, tended him during the passage, and only yielded up his charge when Death met him at the door of the hospital, which promised care and comfort for the boy.

For ten days, Teddy had shivered or burned with fever and ague, pining the while for Kit, and refusing to be comforted, because he had not been able to thank him for the generous protection, which, perhaps, had cost the giver's life. The vivid dream had wrung the childish heart with a fresh pang, and when I tried the solace fitted for his years, the remorseful fear that haunted him found vent in a fresh burst of tears, as he looked at the wasted hands I was endeavoring to warm:

"Oh! If I'd only been as thin when Kit carried me as I am now, maybe he wouldn't have died; but I was heavy, he was hurt worser than we knew, and so it killed him; and I didn't see him to say good-by."

This thought had troubled him in secret; and my assurance that his friend would probably have died at all events, hardly assuaged the bitterness of his regretful grief.

Noncombatants grieve, too, like the little drummer boy, guilt-ridden that he may have contributed to the death of the soldier who saved him.

But this topic goes beyond literary generalities, including a job that few people would want: Mortuary Affairs. Their function is to do just what you think: prepare the bodies of the dead for return to their families. They're usually not trained morticians, just ordinary people doing their job. The HBO film *Taking Chance*, gives you a glimpse into the procedures and traditions for handling the bodies of our military dead. That treatment is every bit as respectful as you would hope.

Charlotte Brock was a Marine lieutenant at Camp Victory, Kuwait and Camp Taqaddum, Iraq in 2004. Her job was to identify and prepare the bodies, which included assembling body parts, cleaning them and inventorying personal effects. She took care of them as if they were her own children. It became a calling for her, a caretaker who treated the fallen with love and respect. She took the words of a hymn – "I will hold your people in my heart" – very seriously. Now back in the states, she explains:

> Part of me wishes I was still with them. Part of me feels that is where I should be: wiping away the blood and grime from a young man's face so that his fellow soldiers can come tell us, "Yes, it's him."

Chaplains

It's not clear who first observed "there are no atheists in foxholes". It's been attributed to World War II war correspondent Ernie Pyle. There are undoubtedly some who would argue with the sentiment. Either way, military chaplains serve all the military, whether they are of the same faith tradition or no faith at all. They are there, on the front lines, to meet the spiritual and emotional needs of their troops.

H. Clay Trumbull served as chaplain of the Tenth Regiment of Connecticut Volunteers during the Civil War. In his memoir, *War Memories of an Army Chaplain*, he offers an interesting perspective on his job description:

> The position of a regimental chaplain was unique. He was a commissioned officer, yet without command. No question of relative rank brought him into rivalry with any other officer. He could be welcomed by a major-general or by a second

> lieutenant without the fear of any seeming incongruity of association, if only he had the power of making himself personally or socially agreeable or useful. Yet he could be among the enlisted men as one entirely with them in sympathy, without any thought on the part of either that he was stepping out of his sphere or crossing the line which divided commissioned officers as a class from enlisted men as a class.

Few civilians consider the issue of rank. Chaplains are sometimes referred to as "officers without troops", meaning they have no one to command. But by virtue of their job description, they are trusted, by officers and enlisted men who may otherwise be wary of confiding in their superiors.

War was different in Trumbull's time. The battlefields were defined, as were the formations. Fighting was mainly conducted on foot or on horseback. When the fighting ended – with battles lasting for days – the ground was soaked with the blood of thousands of the dead. Burying them was important, not just because of hygiene (more men died in the Civil War of infections and illnesses than battle wounds), but because of the need to honor their comrades. Leaving a body to be desecrated by scavengers or by animals is the height of indignity. When soldiers talk of leaving no one behind, they also mean the dead.

Trumbull tells of leading men in burials and prayers whenever there was a lull in the action, even when bombs whistled overhead. When so many are dead, how does the mind react? For this chaplain, after a soldier was shot in the face less than six feet away from him, the answer became deeply personal:

> To say that two thousand or twenty thousand men are killed in a great battle, or that a thousand of the dead are buried in one great trench, produces only a vague impression on the mind at the fullest. There is too much in this to be truly personal to you. But to know one man who is shot down by your side, and to aid in burying him, while his comrades stand with you above his open grave, is a more real matter to you than the larger piece of astounding information.

Wisconsin native Father Matt Foley became a chaplain in a roundabout way. Called to the priesthood while at Marquette University, he was ordained in 1989 and assigned to a parish on the west side of Chicago where he spent five years, followed by six years in Mexico. In 2006, he returned to Chicago to preside over the funeral of Pfc. Daniel Zizumbo, killed by a makeshift bomb in Afghanistan, and whose parents were former parishioners.

Though Foley's brother and roommate both served in the Army, and his uncle had been an Army chaplain in Vietnam, it was the sacrifice of Pfc. Zizumbo that prompted Foley to enlist. There has been a shortage of Catholic priests in the military for some time, reflecting the general shortage of priests in society. That became a motivating factor, too. Exactly two years after the young soldier's death, Foley was sworn in by his brother, a lieutenant colonel.

Foley felt pretty well prepared for war. He wasn't a teenager: he'd been a priest for 19 years, and had experience working with the violence and death that affects young people in Chicago and Mexico.

Still, he told me, no one was out to get him on the West Side of Chicago. War was different: "The cross on your head doesn't protect you there." He was as disconcerted as anyone else to hear incoming missiles.

His day was typical of that of any chaplain: saying four or five masses, including one in Spanish, as well as visiting patients at the hospital in Bagram, and anointing the sick. He wasn't burying the dead, like Trumbull, but he was involved whenever there was a casualty.

Ideally, he said, the commander notifies the unit of a death (if not already known). But because the situation on the front is always fluid, it's not a perfect process. The commander brings the chaplain in to counsel the survivors. The body is blessed, sent to Germany and then on to the US. A formal, standard ceremony is held. It's very controlled, by the book.

The procedure and standardization can be comforting, but they don't ease the grief. Although there had been a relatively new push for a full spectrum of health support (including psychiatrist and counselor) at Bagram, there were other complications in helping the men and women he worked with process their grief. The challenge, Foley insisted, is that our society in general does not do death very well.

We don't give people a chance to mourn, he insisted: in fact we avoid grief and the messy feelings associated with it. Many of the soldiers Foley knew had never been to a funeral in civilian life. Young people come into the service without the life experience of dealing with grief, from a society that avoids talking about it because it's "depressing." They now have to accept their friend's death, while necessarily waiting to process it, probably experiencing more deaths in the meantime. No wonder young soldiers have a hard time.

Survivor guilt was very common, Foley said. He noticed that when there had been a large number of losses, the survivors could be very, very quiet. That's when his work began, keeping an eye on those who were unable to talk about their feelings, being there for them, encouraging them to tell their stories.

Chaplains must confront a wide range of emotions in the men and women they serve: grief, anger, frustration, guilt. They're even, as Foley explained, teaching them how to mourn their friends.

One chaplain, Lt. Col. Doug Etter of the Pennsylvania National Guard, created a ritual to help his troops as they prepared to leave Iraq behind them, a ritual of forgiveness:

> At the end of as brutal 12-month combat tour in Iraq, one battalion chaplain (Etter) gathered the troops and handed out slips of paper. He asked the soldiers to jot down everything they were sorry for, ashamed of, angry about or regretted. The papers went into a makeshift stone baptismal font, and as the soldiers stood silently in a circle, the papers burned to ash.

But any of these chaplains will probably tell you that these ceremonies are as much for them as for their troops.

"Through the Gates of Hell for a Wounded Marine"

They spend each day covered in blood, and every night grieving for those they couldn't save. These are our 'Medics', half soldier half saint.

This description by Theodore Knell, author of *A Hell for Heroes: A SAS Hero's Journey to the Heart of Darkness*, portrays an admiration typical of those who appreciate what medics' jobs are like. Those of us who grew up watching *M.A.S.H.* and *Combat!* and *Mr. Roberts* saw characterizations of medical personnel as either older and Yoda-like, or irreverent, hard-drinking womanizers. They were doctors and medics, with the occasional nurse to tempt them. Moving up with those who were fighting, though at the rear of battle, they might even be in danger at times, but that big red cross on the roof generally protected them from harm.

However true those depictions may have been at the time, medicine has changed dramatically since the wars in

Afghanistan and Iraq began. Survival rates are higher, but soldiers are returning home with more catastrophic injuries. Traumatic brain injury (TBI) is the most common injury, affecting roughly 60,000 returning troops from those wars, according to the Department of Defense.

Commander Richard Jadick's *On Call in Hell: A Doctor's Iraq War Story* is a powerful first-hand account of his military career, focusing on eight months spent in Iraq with the First Battalion, Eighth Marines (the 1/8) of the Second Marine Division. His account of the Battle of Fallujah in November, 2004, marked the first time he and fellow battalion surgeon Will Dutton put a new theory into practice: the Forward Aid Station.

Let's back up for a moment and consider how casualties were handled on the battlefield before Fallujah.

Just like in the movies and TV shows we've watched, in real life medical personnel are stationed at a battalion aid station at the rear of a war zone, near headquarters, where they could be safe. As a rule, they aren't responsible for their own security, though they are allowed to fire if fired upon, in self-defense or to protect their patients. Their safety must be provided by others.

The wounded are brought to the BAS for level-one care – everything but surgery. The more seriously wounded patients are transported directly from the battlefield to a level-two facility, in other words, a surgical unit or a hospital. Often, as Jadick observed, the BAS was so far back that it was bypassed in favor of the hospitals.

Jadick and Dutton saw the obvious gap: the battlefield itself. If battalion leadership could establish mobile headquarters (called Jump Command Posts), why couldn't they create a jump aid station? It was a simple theory. Jadick explains:

> When a man is wounded on the battlefield, there are three possible outcomes. He can be killed, instantly or within minutes. Or he can be more or less fine – cut, bruised or punctured in a way that may be debilitating but won't threaten his life, even if he doesn't get medical treatment for hours or more. And then there is the vast middle ground of wounds where timely medical intervention will mean the difference between that Marine flying home in a seat or in a box.

It was that vast middle ground that the medical personnel of the 1/8 were trying to address. They would set up a jump aid station that would include a surgical unit right on the front lines. They could stabilize the most seriously wounded before the medevac helicopters could safely airlift them to the hospital. They could prevent unnecessary discomfort and possibly save lives. It was a simple idea. And given the Second Marine Division corpsmen's motto – "through the gates of hell for a wounded Marine" – it made perfect sense. But would it work?

The Battle of Fallujah was one of the most important battles of the Iraq War. When it was over, the 1/8 (which was made up of 1,000 soldiers) lost 21 killed in action and another 200 were wounded in action. Those numbers, though tragic, paled in comparison to the 30-40% casualty rate predicted before the battle. If time is truly of the essence, as Jadick insists, then the Forward Aid Station certainly contributed to the low number of those killed.

Jadick and his crew learned from the ones who didn't make it, and sometimes what they learned helped save the next one. That was not necessarily a comforting thought on the eve of battle.

> I remember sitting there and looking around, wondering who they would be. These were guys I had known for months now, as well as guys I had just linked up with in the last couple of days...*this must be what the colonel feels like about everybody*, I remember thinking...I couldn't help but feel a little guilty and overwhelmed. I had become close with some of these people and I had to remind myself that I was a doctor and an officer – I had to keep the personal out of it and do what was best for the battalion.

Jadick, speaks with great affection for corpsmen, too, the medical personnel working alongside him, who are often forgotten, but who hold the most decorated rating in the US Navy, with twenty-two Medals of Honor.

> The cumulative brutality of the injuries we were seeing was starting to have an effect. The corpsmen were no older than the Marines we were treating – eighteen, nineteen, maybe twenty-three years old at the most – and they were seeing things that would floor an experienced trauma surgeon. And the corpsmen were often treating people they knew well, friends they had trained with for years in some cases, an emotional punch that civilian medical personnel rarely have to face. Sometimes

> wounded Marines would be carried in and the corpsmen wouldn't even recognize them; they were coming in so messed up, covered in blood and gunk and mud. Then they'd see the man's name on his dog tags, and you could see the pain in their eyes as the realization sank in.

Because women were not exposed to life-threatening situations – at least not officially – their own experiences with grief and survivor guilt have not been given the attention they deserve. Some of that guilt was about sending their patients back out into the field. The nurses did their jobs – helped their patients heal – only to watch them leave, and in some cases, return with new wounds.

Anne Simon Auger was an Army nurse who served in the 91st Evacuation Hospital at Chu Lai, South Vietnam in 1969. Her admitted naïveté soon gave way to an emotional self-defense adopted by many who served.

> I found I'd built up walls real effectively. I was patient and tender with the GIs…I was very professional, but I was distant. I worry sometimes about the way I treated those GIs in intensive care…Because of the walls I'd put up I didn't listen to them, didn't hear what they might be trying to tell me even just in gestures or whatever. I wasn't open to them because I was so closed to myself.

Her response was not unusual. Everyone in battle has to shut off a part of themselves in order to function, including doctors, nurses and medics. They must focus on others, rather than themselves, encouraging others to work through their grief. As a result, their own grief must be put on hold.

The medics in Kelly Kennedy's book *They Fought For Each Other: The Triumph and Tragedy of the Hardest Hit Unit in Iraq* created a physical space so that no one could isolate themselves.

> The medics took on the brunt of the mental health work, and they watched out for each other. Most of the men tried to create some sort of privacy in their living areas, but the medics did the opposite: They tore down the walls. They had a room inside the aid station, and they pushed their bunk beds up against the walls, leaving a communal middle area where they played card games, cleaned their weapons, and talked about what they'd seen that day. They couldn't talk about it with anybody else without hurting them. The medics dealt with more blood and death and pain than the troops did, and the grunts tried to make up for that in the best way they knew how: constant teasing.

It was a safe place, an escape in the middle of hell. Only in such a safe, supportive environment could they begin to process their grief. They also developed coping mechanisms.

> But Holladay knew the worst was still coming. He and Guenther and Whelchel and Hendrix and the other medics would identify the dead and fill out the paperwork. Holladay would look in to the faces of his friends, and those faces would remain

> forever a snapshot in his memory. He would smell burned flesh.
>
> But he wouldn't share those memories with his friends. He would build a fortress around them; he would remind himself that it was a privilege to spend that last bit of time with his friends; he would talk to the other medics about what they'd seen and what they'd felt.

Journalists Sebastian Junger and Tim Hetherington were embedded for a year in Afghanistan, and from that experience created an award-winning documentary. Like me, you may have assumed the name, *Restrepo*, came from a location or battle in Afghanistan. But it didn't.

Early in the deployment, medic Juan Restrepo was shot and died on the way to a hospital. He was 20 years old. His death shook up the platoon, in no small part because as the medic, he was the person others went to for support. When they set up their camp, they named it for him.

Embedded

As long as there have been wars, there have been people reporting on war. Though Herodotus wrote an account of the Persian Wars, he wasn't there. So the history of the Peloponnesian Wars was probably the first eye-witness account of warfare by a war correspondent.

Some correspondents were recruited by the government for propaganda purposes: to report on (and often embellish) good news from the front so that support for the war would remain strong at home. They might represent newspapers, magazines, television, radio or internet sites. While some had an agenda – to promote a particular point of view – all were looking for a way to convey the truth of war to those not in the middle of it. Katherine Skiba, a reporter sent by the Department of Defense, describes the challenge all have faced:

> There is no way I can prepare someone who has never witnessed combat for the shock of the first

> sight of a badly wounded soldier, screaming in pain, begging for his mother. Or the sight of the face of a young soldier in death – a soldier of either side. You will learn to process the images and move on and do your job. But what you see in battle will never leave you.

For centuries, accounts of wars around the world were written and published weeks or months later. It wasn't until the telegraph was invented that same-day news could be transmitted from the front lines to the home front. Telegrams meant the world knew what was happening on the battlefield in real time, no delays.

Until World War II, news from the front came in newspaper or radio reports, days or even weeks later. Whereas telegraphed news was necessarily brief and to the point, the language in these accounts was flowery and emotional, meant to keep up the morale of the people on the home front. Some of those correspondents were famous, like Edward R. Murrow or Ernie Pyle, killed on Okinawa just six days after the death of President Franklin D. Roosevelt.

Reporting changed dramatically as visuals began to rule the day. The newsreel, a popular feature at movie theatres before the advent of television, enabled the government and other news entities to report on the war in a new way. Now, instead of just words, civilians could see what was happening. Again, it wasn't instantaneous, and it was not without its own propaganda purposes, but the ability to see the horrors of war was something dramatically different.

The Vietnam War was the first "living room war", by virtue of the ability of news organizations to report nightly on what had happened earlier that day. You may recall, as I do, watching the beginning of Desert Storm on CNN. The advent of cable news – and later, the internet – meant we now have instantaneous access. The viewer was now a (passive) participant.

Censorship has always been an issue. The famous film director John Huston created a series for the US government during World War II that was not shown, because it was not "upbeat" enough. During the early days of the wars in Iraq and Afghanistan, the media were prohibited from showing footage of planes, bearing the bodies of those who had been killed, arriving at Dover Air Force Base.

Journalists feel a strong sense of responsibility to the troops they have come to know and respect. When they're prevented from telling the truth – or the whole truth, including the grief they feel themselves and witness in others – they also feel an additional sense of guilt for having let down their friends. When the news is censored, those of us at home can't fully appreciate the enormity of the personal loss.

Just like reporting changed, so did the way wars are conducted. Long gone are the battlefields of old, with clearly defined borders and conduct. Now the enemy is everywhere, fighting with explosives hidden from view or disguised as something benign.

That makes being an embedded reporter today very different: reporters take on the same challenges and dangers as those who are fighting. According to Reporters Without Borders, over 1,100 journalists have been killed since 1992, 39% of them in war zones.

Skiba and other reporters are there to do their jobs. But in her book, *Sister in the Band of Brothers: Embedded with the*

101st Airborne in Iraq, she urges those in her shoes to help when possible, to not forget that before you are a reporter, you are a human being.

Her training included bits of information like "don't pick up anything strange" that could blow up in your face, don't sit down near a military vehicle or it might run over you: practical suggestions that would keep her safe. But she couldn't do her job without earning the trust and respect of the soldiers she lived with. That meant she had to identify with them, not other reporters. She had to tough it out: no whining, no excuses.

Her job – whether she realized it at first or not – was not to report on the war, but rather on those fighting the war, as one officer reminded her.

> The average enlisted soldier, he predicted, initially would find a journalist "an item of curiosity" and be interested in how we do our jobs and where our reports are published. "In a day or two you become, in his eyes, 'our goddamn reporter,' spoken with pride, not ridicule. You are the only civilian he will see in the field in a combat zone. You are a sign to him that someone outside the big green machine cares how he lives and how he dies. Do care. At the same time, be aware that the GI, the grunt, has a perverse and often black sense of humor. He will pull your chain given the opportunity."

That meant she had to get close to them, make friends with them. She wasn't charged with reporting on numbers and strategy: she was charged with telling the stories of the men and women who were putting their lives on the line. That would, hopefully, make the people at home sympathetic towards and supportive of the war effort.

But it also meant that Skiba – and Sebastian Junger and Tim Hetherington and others embedded with the troops – must walk a fine line: doing their jobs with all the professionalism and training they possess, while caring for people who could be killed at any moment.

Army Times writer Kelly Kennedy was embedded with Charlie Company 1-26 in Iraq. In her appropriately titled book, *They Fought For Each Other*, Kennedy tells the stories of the 138 men who would earn at least 95 combat medals, including the Medal of Honor.

While the number of commendations may seem high, they were not her focus. She, too, found that the men of Charlie 1-26 were not there for glory. Instead, she introduces young men like the one who threw himself on a grenade to save his friends, and the medics who struggled with grief even as they counseled their men.

Sebastian Junger and Tim Hetherington spent a year embedded with a platoon in the Korengal Valley of Afghanistan. Junger's book *War*, as well as the documentary they co-directed, *Restrepo*, give powerful first-hand accounts of what it's like not just for the soldiers they cover, but for the correspondents themselves. The two friends were not together the entire year. Both suffered injuries and went home to recuperate, but kept coming back to keep their commitment.

Junger was interviewed by Terry Gross for "Fresh Air" on NPR in 2013, in conjunction with the HBO premiere of Junger's documentary tribute to Hetherington *Which Way is the Front Line From Here?* He describes what it was like for Hetherington when he filmed the death of one of the soldiers. It wasn't Hetherington's first war, nor the first time witnessing the death of someone he knew; in Liberia a rebel fighter carrying his gear was killed. But his camera continued rolling as the men struggled to reclaim the body of their comrade in Afghanistan.

> Well, he is in tears because he felt guilty that he'd filmed it. And there's a difference between seeing someone else die and filming it, and filming the reaction of the people who loved him. But he understood that the soldiers were glad he was there. It wasn't that, you know, there was a tense moment with a guy who didn't know him. The guy who yelled at him was in a different unit and they later became friends. But, so it wasn't a problem with the guys who were there, they wanted us there, you know. It was an internal problem. It was a moral problem, like, you are making your living documenting the pain of other people. And even though it's a good thing to do and a necessary thing to do, it creates moral confusion in a person, in a sensitive person. And Tim was incredibly sensitive and it took him a long time to work through that.

Survivor guilt was something Junger didn't understand when he was in Afghanistan. He spoke of a soldier who felt guilty for not preventing the death of a buddy, even though that soldier died instantly after being shot in the forehead. No one could've prevented it. No one could've saved him. But logic didn't matter: he still felt guilty.

Jungle struggled for the first time with guilt after Hetherington was killed in Libya in 2011: for not being with his friend, for not being able to save him, for being alive. He thought back to the soldier above.

> When Tim got killed I understood it completely.

We think of war correspondents as tough, professional risk-takers almost emotionless in their jobs. But they are as susceptible to grief and guilt after a friend dies as anyone who picks up a weapon. We just don't see what happens to them when the cameras stop rolling.

"Never Shall I Fail My Comrades" – Guilt

The most common problem experienced by Marines due to unhealed grief is survivor guilt, which may last a long time.

This, again, is taken from the US Marines *Leaders Guide for Managing Marines in Distress*, but it applies to every branch of the military. It can apply to civilians, too, though the reasons for that guilt rarely rise to the level of the survivor guilt felt in this situation. A clinical psychologist in the VA San Francisco Health System reported that 80% of the veterans she saw experienced the wounding or death of a friend. And the guilt can last for decades.

Survivor guilt is not grief. It's a factor in complicated grief, but it's not grief. It's a very complex, illogical response that includes self-doubt, second-guessing and a belief that the wrong person died.

What's illogical about believing that your friend should've

survived instead of you? Perhaps nothing, but even those who can objectively reach the conclusion that they couldn't have changed the outcome will torture themselves with "what if"s.

While writing this book, a prayer popped into my head, a Catholic prayer, the Confiteor:

> I confess to almighty God and to you, my brothers and sisters, that I have greatly sinned, in my thoughts and in my words, in what I have done and in what I have failed to do, through my fault, through my fault, through my most grievous fault...

While this prayer may not occur word for word to the people suffering from survivor guilt, it is the essence of what they feel.

Death is hard for people to accept, whether it's the death of a family member or a close friend. Death is even hard for those in the middle of war, where death is sudden, violent and all too commonplace. But one of the things that makes it hardest for men and women in the military to grieve is the belief that they could somehow have saved their friend.

One of the soldiers in David Finkel's book, *Thank You For Your Service*, tells of the persistent dream that his friend, Harrelson, is on fire, demanding, "Why didn't you save me?" Another veteran, Christopher Golembe, remembers that after James Doster was killed, he told his friend Adam, "None of this shit would have happened if you were there." When Adam heard the words meant as a compliment, he felt only overwhelming guilt.

Sebastian Junger observed that even the medics – renowned for their bravery under fire – were terrified of not being able to save the lives of their friends.

Theodore Knell speaks eloquently of facing one's own mortality after the death of a close friend in battle in his memoir *A Hell for Heroes: A SAS Hero's Journey to the Heart of Darkness*. And while his reflections on survivor guilt are from the Falklands – a conflict much smaller than Iraq or Afghanistan or either World War – the sentiment echoes those of soldiers before and since:

> But when the fight is over, whether you're standing over the mass grave of your fallen brothers at Goose Green, or alongside the coffin of a fallen comrade in the peace and quiet of the regimental church, for those of us who remain, there is nowhere left to hide…
>
> Every death is accompanied by an enormous feeling of guilt in those of us who are left behind. This is the guilt from having been there, but surviving…There was always the feeling that maybe I could have done more, even prevented it from happening in some way. Maybe even the loss of my own life would have been preferable to the guilt I felt at such times…
>
> It doesn't matter how long you spend around death, or how many friends you lose. On the contrary, the impact of each new event will be even greater than the one before, and those feelings of guilt will just grow stronger. Guilt hits you even when you weren't there. I was 5,000 miles away when my best friend was killed in an ambush, but I felt totally ashamed of myself for not being there with him, for letting him down, leaving

him to die alone when he needed me the most.

The spiral of finding fault and assuming blame cannot end until the soldier can do one very important thing: forgive him/herself for surviving. Then someday they can find the solace that Ernie Pyle described in his report from Tunisia in 1943 for *Stars and Stripes*:

> This is our war, and we will carry it with us as we go on from one battlefield to another until it is all over, leaving some of us behind on every beach, in every field. We are just beginning with the ones who lie back of us here in Tunisia. I don't know whether it was their good fortune or their misfortune to get out of it so early in the game. I guess it doesn't make any difference, once a man has gone. Medals and speeches and victories are nothing to them anymore. They died and others lived and nobody knows why it is so. They died and thereby the rest of us can go on and on. When we leave here for the next shore, there is nothing we can do for the ones beneath the wooden crosses, except perhaps to pause and murmur, "Thanks, pal."

PTSD and Moral Injury

It may seem like a very recent phenomenon, but PTSD (Post-Traumatic Stress Disorder) is not new. During the War of 1812, Napoleon's field surgeons reported on combat stress. It was "soldier's heart" in the Civil War. By World War I, the psychological and neurological effects of war were identified as "shell shock", which became known as "traumatic war neurosis" or "battle fatigue" after World War II.

People often assume that World War II veterans, "The Greatest Generation", did not suffer from the effects of war like today's military. I remember watching the 1963 film *Captain Newman, M.D.* with Gregory Peck as a World War II psychiatrist treating soldiers suffering from a variety of disorders: survivor guilt, flashbacks, anger, delusions, nightmares. Granted, I was a kid, but I assumed it was fiction: World War II soldiers were strong and focused, not haunted by what they'd done during the war. So I was surprised to discover later that the film was inspired by Leo Rosten's 1963 novel, which was based on the story of his close friend Ralph Greenson, a Captain in the US Army Medical Corps, one of the first in his field to associate PTSD with wartime experiences.

Thomas Childers' *Soldiers From the War Returning: The Greatest Generation's Troubled Homecoming from World War II* looks at the challenges, largely forgotten today, that faced veterans returning from that war:

> Roughly 1.3 million service personnel suffered some kind of psychological setback during World War II. By July 1943, the U.S. Army was discharging ten thousand men each month for psychiatric reasons, and the numbers increased as the war dragged on. During the Battle of Okinawa, fought between late March and the end of June 1945, the marines suffered twenty thousand psychiatric casualties. Woefully understaffed Veterans Administration (now the Department of Veterans Affairs, or VA) hospitals were swamped with "psychoneurotic" cases, and two years after the war's end, half the patients in VA medical facilities were men suffering from "invisible wounds." Post-traumatic stress disorder was not diagnosed until 1980, but in the aftermath of the Second World War, depression, recurring nightmares, survivor guilt, outbursts of rage (most frequently directed at family members), "exaggerated startled responses," and anxiety reactions – all of which are recognized today as classic symptoms of PTSD – were as common as they were unnerving. With few psychiatrists to treat them and a cultural ethos that hardly encouraged

open discussion of emotional problems, especially among men, many veterans simply suffered in private – often with devastating consequences for them and their families.

It wasn't until 1980 that PTSD first appeared in the *Diagnostic and Statistical Manual of Mental Disorders (DSM-III)*. But the general public was already attached to the myth of the "crazy Vietnam vet". The idea that those who fought in previous wars were "better" men – a belief that created a stigma that lasts to this day. Part of the ethos of "The Greatest Generation" is that World War II veterans did their jobs without regret, and left the war behind them. We consider them heroes – and rightly so. But they too were vulnerable to the same challenges as those who fought before and since.

The strain of re-deployments to Iraq and Afghanistan in the past few years has made the prevalence of PTSD diagnoses news. Those who were diagnosed with some level of PTSD (and there are gradations) were met with skepticism, because the numbers were soaring. But so were the numbers of suicides, by active duty and veterans, now almost two dozen every day.

None of this means that those suffering from PTSD are doomed to commit suicide or horrific crimes. In the aftermath of the April, 2014 mass shooting at Fort Hood, Dakota Meyer, the youngest recipient of the Medal of Honor, argued against the media's immediate assumption that the killing spree was the result of PTSD. It was not only inflammatory, Meyer said, but it could potentially discourage someone from seeking treatment.

Grief – particularly the unresolved/delayed grief already mentioned – is a contributing factor, but not the only major factor. We often hear of veterans affected by triggers such as 4th of July fireworks, sounds that take them back to the battlefield, reliving the horrific events they can't forget. The typical symptoms are that startle reflex, memory loss, fear and flashbacks. Though more than 50,000 veterans of Iraq and Afghanistan have been diagnosed with PTSD, five times that number are believed to be affected by what is now called moral injury.

Moral injury occurs when a person violates their own moral beliefs, and believes that that violation means they are no longer a decent human being.

William P. Nash was a combat psychiatrist who counseled soldiers after the 2004 Battle of Fallujah. The trauma expressed by those he saw was never about fear, though the fighting was especially horrific. It was about moral injury and survivor guilt. It was never about what happened to them, but what they did or failed to do for others, including the failure to save their battle buddies.

Not all moral injury is about grieving the death of a battle buddy. Some is about making mistakes in the field, questioning the morality of an order, killing women and children, no matter how justified.

It's easy, then to confuse veterans suffering from moral injury with those suffering from PTSD. Moral injury presents itself in sorrow, grief, regret, shame and alienation. The symptoms it shares in common with PTSD include anger, depression, anxiety, insomnia, nightmares and self-medication with drugs and/or alcohol. You can suffer from both, but they are two different disorders. Where specific forms of therapy (including drugs) can effectively treat PTSD, they do not work with those suffering from moral injury.

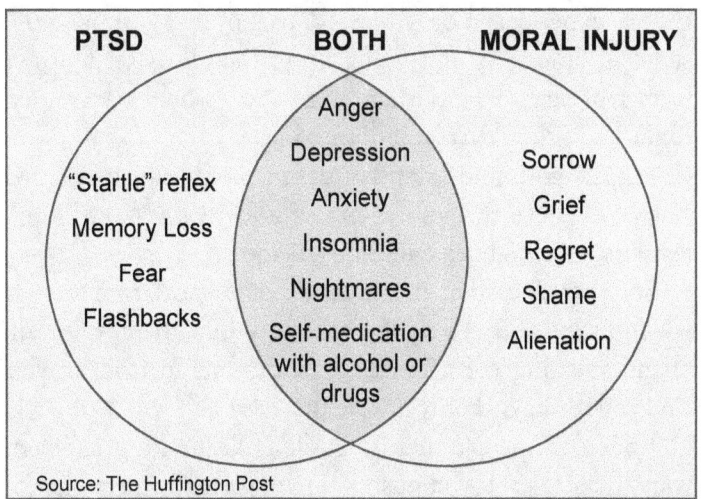
Source: The Huffington Post

You will be hard pressed to find anyone in the Department of Defense or branches of the military who will discuss moral injury. Their jobs are to prepare men and women for battle, and in that, they do an excellent job. You join the military to obey orders and carry out your mission. The bad stuff, well, it's just part of it.

There is one small program at the San Diego Naval Medical Center that shows promise, but much more is needed to help veterans confront their moral injuries and heal from them. Why only one? The science behind the treatment is still developing and the government and the military bureaucracies can be slow to change. Remember how long it took to admit the effects of Vietnam veterans' exposure to Agent Orange?

The whole concept of moral injury attacks the very nature of war. Men and women are asked to put their lives on the line for a cause greater than themselves, with the understanding that they will have to do things that are only acceptable in that setting. When people feel guilt over what they've experienced or witnessed, part of that guilt is in the sense of failure for not living up to the ideals set by their branch of service: I did what I had to do – what I was trained to do – so I shouldn't let it bother me.

But the guilt and grief that define moral injury have led Nash to believe that moral injury underlies veteran homelessness, criminal behavior and suicide.

So what does that mean? You come back from war. If you're lucky, you get eight weeks of group therapy to talk about watching your friends blown to bits in front of you. And you're okay? If only it were that easy.

I often tell people that if you don't deal with grief when your friend dies, if you push it down, pretend you're okay, it will come back to bite you in the butt. The grief will be worse, and it will be more difficult to deal with. But I can't say that to people in the military.

They have little choice but to push down their grief, despite policies in place for implementation of counseling in the best of all possible worlds. Rarely does anyone lose just one friend. The losses mount up: sometimes multiple deaths the same day, sometimes a series of deaths, sometimes both. You can't hit a pause button on the war but you have to with your grief.

The effects, as we've seen here, are serious and long lasting. According to a 2004 study of Vietnam veterans by Ilona Pivar at the National Center for PTSD at the VA in Palo Alto, California, the grief felt over a losing a combat buddy was comparable, more than 30 years later, to that of losing a spouse in the previous six months.

Grief that intense, thirty years later, cannot be dismissed out of hand as a simple internal conflict. It's a testament to the strength of those friendships, and the ongoing difficulties faced by our military when they try to work through that grief.

Suicide

We've reached a time where more military die from suicide than from battle. "It's an epidemic," said Secretary of Defense Leon Panetta, testifying before Congress in the summer of 2012. "Something is wrong." At this writing, twenty-two veterans and one active duty soldier commit suicide every day.

Hundreds of books, thousands of discussions have considered the question of why people commit suicide. Again, it's not a new phenomenon. But the numbers are still shocking.

Experts have pointed to issues that were present before enlistment: substance abuse, fascination with guns, undiagnosed mental illness, family dysfunction, unrealistic expectations of military life, fixation on being a "hero". In fact, a 2014 study published in the *Journal of the American Medical Association* finds that 1 in 5 active duty military had undiagnosed mental illness at the time of enlistment.

Not only enlisted personnel can develop problems during deployment. The strain of leadership – of not only the responsibility for commanding their unit but of being a role model – can lead to unrealistic expectations. The leader might believe they can forego basic human needs as they demand perfection of themselves.

One of the most horrific passages in Kelly Kennedy's book is the story of a sergeant who spirals out of control. Denying himself rest, he's finally ordered to get more sleep, but refuses: he believes taking the time to sleep might make him appear weak to his men. Then he stops drinking water in 107 degree heat, obsessing that if he did, there would none left for his men. His mental condition spiraled downward until the terrible day he killed himself in front of those men.

The demographics are sobering:

> Nearly 1 in 5 suicides nationally is a veteran

> The suicide rate for veterans is twice the national average for civilians, perhaps triple.

> 69% of veterans who commit suicide are 50 years or older.

Here's why the number of veterans committing suicide each day – 22 – might actually be much higher:

> Not all veteran suicides are reported as such. Military status may not be included in the death certificate.

> "Suicide by cop" – people who provoke police into killing them – is not included.

> A February 2013 Veterans Administration study that came up with the 22-a-day figure was based on data from only 22 states. That means it can reasonably be assumed that this number is low by at least half.

Theodore Knell believes the burdens of combat can weigh heavily enough to lead to suicide, even years later.

> Since the end of the Falklands War far more soldiers have committed suicide as a result of what they experienced than were killed during the actual fighting. The war cemetery at Port Stanley holds the remains of those who fell in battle, but the children of the islanders have now dedicated a new area alongside it called the 'Suicides' Graveyard'. Each new death is commemorated by the planting of a tree with the name below. And while that first graveyard remains at a constant number, the 'other' graveyard is growing steadily as the conflict continues to kill its victims. Over the years the sense of loss slowly softens and we lean towards the happier times we spent with these men. I used to wander the Brecon Beacons for days on end, alone, just following the routes we once walked together. But no matter how far I walked, the guilt would always be there, and still is.

Does it make sense that guilt could last so long? It does to people who, like Ted Janis, are haunted by one stanza in particular from the Ranger Creed, motto of the US Army Rangers.

Never shall I fail my comrades.

Janis, in a story that appeared in *The Daily Beast*, believed he was well trained to expect and deal with the deaths of friends in combat. What no one prepared him for was that his friends would continue to die after returning home – from suicide.

He became well-versed on the facts: 22 veterans take their life every day; suicides occur in clusters, with one often influencing the next; many who consider suicide do so in isolation, never seeking help. Government programs and medical personnel try to identify those at risk, but many still on duty are reluctant to come forward to seek help, believing it will negatively impact their careers.

Once discharged, it's easy to fall through the cracks. Janis, though, puts forward a compelling case: that veterans can save each other – indeed, that veterans themselves are the best suited to save their friends.

> And so, to my fellow veterans: Reach out. There is support waiting for your call. At my friend's funeral, over twenty old Army buddies came in to grieve, from New York City, West Point, D.C., Colorado, Tennessee. All of us would have done anything we could to have saved our friend. If only he had asked.

Brian Kinsella – of Stop Soldier Suicide – also believes that the key to prevention is to get to those at risk when they're first discharged. His organization is entirely made up of veterans – staff and volunteers.

Their philosophy is, first, that this is a decades-long mission. There are no quick fixes or simple solutions. Every member of the military at risk for suicide must be helped in an efficient, appropriate and individual manner. And the numbers of those at risk are growing.

Second, veterans are in the best position to help other veterans. "Leave no one behind" is as strong a belief after the war is over as it is on the front lines. In fact, Kinsella believes the war isn't over as long as there are men and women veterans who need help.

This is their approach, as outlined on their website:

> **1. Initial Contact**: Active and Veteran Service members contact us through a local chapter, our Facebook page, a 24-hour hotline or chat feature (via our Contact Center coming soon) or other partner organizations.
>
> **2. Assess & "Triage"**: We talk with the person or family member contacting us to determine the urgency of the care needed and the right course to take. It's important for us to understand the situation so we can get the best help available, the RIGHT help, for the Soldier or Veteran.
>
> **3. Transition & Follow Up**: We connect the person in need to one of many resources, whether that be mental health professionals, local chapter support, partner organizations or other resources that can provide care and assistance.

The people at Stop Soldier Suicide are not from the government, nor are they mental health professionals. The simple and powerful truth is that they've been there – they speak the same language as those they're pledged to help – and can direct them towards the resources they need.

As is often the case in civilian suicides, nearly half of those who die by suicide in the military community had not been seen by a mental health professional in the three months prior. The stigma surrounding mental illness in society is intensified in a military setting, whether active duty or veterans.

Suicide is the great unknown. Those left behind struggle for meaning, for answers that will never come. They are frustrated and angry and depressed, and why wouldn't they be?

While Janis's frustration was that his friend didn't reach out for help, assuming a person will reach out when feeling suicidal is unrealistic. It's impossible to accurately predict who will attempt to commit suicide, but social isolation seems to be a compelling warning sign.

Sometimes a soldier or veteran will reach out, only to be frustrated by slow-moving bureaucracy or the dismissiveness of those around them: "Hey, you made it back, that's all that matters," some civilians say.

The complexity and urgency of this problem is why the people you'll hear from next are so important.

Resilience

> What cannot be talked about cannot be put to rest. And if it is not, the wounds will fester from generation to generation. (Bruno Bettelheim)

Resilience is a fancy word, I guess, for what most of us would refer to as coping skills or a positive mental attitude. Bad things happen to good people all the time, but we've all seen those who are unable to move on from them. Sometimes they're temporarily stuck in their grief; sometimes they need help to process it.

Resilience doesn't mean you ignore what happened to you. It doesn't mean you pretend it was no big deal. It means you faced it head-on, and, with the help of those around you, came to terms with your experience and moved on.

Why are some veterans able to process their grief more effectively than others?

They probably have support systems: mental health professionals, battle buddies, chaplains, leaders, all of whom understood what they went through and why the complications of their grief have affected them so deeply.

They had experience. As Father Matt Foley pointed out, many of the young men and women he served with had never been to a funeral before losing a friend in battle.

They were able to express their grief. Grief professionals may disagree on the methods, but all agree that the ability to share the grief is a strong determining factor. We've seen the effects of unresolved or delayed grief – especially in terms of survivor guilt – so now it's time to look at how veterans have found a way to heal.

Therapy directed towards resolving moral injury is a field that's in its infancy. Veterans may be unable to recognize the need for such therapy. And even if they do, they may be unwilling to seek help, fearing stigma or just a reluctance to admit to something they feel is a weakness. Active duty military may fear negative consequences for their careers. But in a safe, welcoming environment, they may be willing to talk or write about their grief.

In the past few years, writing programs for veterans have sprung up at universities, grief support groups, veteran's organizations and websites. Some are professional writing programs, but many are simply therapeutic (whether medically sanctioned or not).

The Red Badge Project in Washington state, founded by actor Tom Skerritt and former Army Capt. Evan Bailey, connects artists with ill, wounded and injured soldiers of the Joint Base Lewis-McChord's Warrior Transition Battalion.

There's Military Experience and the Arts, that works with veterans and their families, to publish *Journal of Military Experience* and *Blue Nostalgia: A Journal of Post-Traumatic Growth*, among others.

These programs encourage veterans – in groups, individually or online – to share the stories they are struggling with. While this trend may be relatively recent, war diaries and post-war memoirs are not.

About fifteen years ago, I was first exposed to the rich tradition of World War I poetry. Much of it comes from the UK and consists of soldiers and veterans telling of their experiences. The language is deeply emotional, especially when recounting stories of losing friends. They speak of their love for their comrades – not a sexual or romantic love, but the love of their fellow soldiers, to whom they owe their lives.

In his World War I diary, *Some Desperate Glory: The World War I Diary of a British Officer*, Edwin Campion Vaughan rightly observes:

> One of the most pathetic features of the war is this continual forming of real friendships which last a week or two, or even months, and are suddenly shattered forever by death…

It is a theme that echoes throughout first-person accounts, poetry and fiction by veterans throughout time.

Oral histories – conducted by organizations such as the Library of Congress, American Women Veterans, StoryCorps, and Pritzker Military Museum and Library – also allow men and women who have served their country the opportunity to share their experiences. Not everyone wants to talk about what happened, except perhaps with those who were with them. That's where groups like the VFW function well, offering a safe, supportive atmosphere to share stories. But the ability to preserve those stories is relatively new and important: to the veteran themselves and their friends and family.

Remember, too, that the inability to immediately process grief adds to the need later to share the stories of their friends, to ensure that they will not be forgotten.

For those who do not feel comfortable talking or writing, visual arts can also provide a therapeutic outlet. The Vietnam Veterans Art Group was founded in Chicago in 1981 and opened its doors as the Vietnam Veterans Art Museum. They broadened their focus to include veterans from all conflicts, and in 2010, became the National Veterans Art Museum. In addition to showcasing works of art by over 250 veterans, they also operate a growing art therapy program called VetCAT (Veterans Creative Art Therapy).

Michael Reagan is a Vietnam veteran living in Seattle who was asked by the widow of a corpsman who died in Iraq to draw a portrait of her husband. The drawing turned out to be so therapeutic for her that Reagan vowed to draw a portrait of every member of the US military killed in Iraq. To date, he has created over 3,500 portraits for the families of those fallen heroes. The work is therapeutic for Reagan, a Vietnam veteran, as well:

> "I don't know why I'm still alive," he said. He can clearly recall the death of a close friend during the 1968 Tet offensive and still regrets not being able to summon a few words of comfort before his friend died.
>
> "He looked right at me and died, and I'll never forget those eyes, so part of what I do when I do my portraits is I always start with the eyes," Reagan said.

It's no surprise that many veterans start organizations to help their battle buddies. Vietnam vet Bob Nevins, who piloted a medical evacuation helicopter for the 101st Airborne, founded Saratoga WarHorse Foundation.

In this program, veterans are paired with horses, training them as they themselves are healed by the process.

> "Taking action is really the key here," said Nevins in an article in *Stars and Stripes*. "Every day you can read in the newspaper, see on television and they're talking about record suicides in the military. What's happening to these young men and women? We all know we can't identify who's going to be the next suicide victim. But what are we going to do about it? The program is designed specifically to deal with that question and to also help engage the community to take action."

There are other programs – dog therapy, music therapy, community service projects such as The Mission Continues. They are spread throughout the US and other countries as well.

The men and women who fight are not the only ones who find that their war experience forces them to take stock of their lives and redefine their purpose.

After Tim Hetherington was killed in Libya in 2011, Sebastian Junger recalled how he responded to the news of his death:

> And within the hour, I decided not to cover combat again. I didn't want to risk traumatizing everyone I loved by getting killed myself.

Making *Which Way is the Front Line From Here?* was a tribute to Hetherington and his passion for documenting war and its effects on young men. But Junger took it a step farther, because Hetherington could have survived his shrapnel wound. He bled out in minutes before he could be transported to the clinic because no one with him – including other journalists – knew first aid.

Junger founded Reporters Instructed in Saving Colleagues (RISC) to train freelancers (who do most of the war reporting) in an intensive, four-day medical training program. It's free of charge, including the kit. The realization that his friend could've survived pushed Junger in an entirely new direction.

The men and women who have experienced war firsthand – those who fight and lead, those who tend to their physical and spiritual needs, and those who tell their stories – have been forever changed by their experiences. Those of us who did not serve with them – or did not serve at all – cannot understand what it was like to lose their friends under those circumstances, try though we may.

All we can do is listen, which is the single most powerful thing anyone can for someone who's grieving the death of a friend. Listen, just listen, without judgment.

Listen to them tell you what they loved about their friends.

Listen to them tell you how they wish they could've changed things.

Listen to them tell you how losing their friends changed their own lives forever.

The fourth stanza of Robert Laurence Binyon's famous World War I poem *For The Fallen* is often quoted at memorial services. That last line in particular is one that is the mantra for many veterans returning from war, indeed for all of us who have lost a friend:

> They shall grow not old, as we that are left grow old:
>
> Age shall not weary them, nor the years condemn.
>
> At the going down of the sun and in the morning
>
> We will remember them.

Acknowledgements

I first want to thank those individuals who were so generous with their time: Don Oleniacz, Westside VA Medical Center, Los Angeles; Father Matt Foley; Jill Harrington-Lamorie, Center for the Study of Traumatic Stress; Brian Kinsella, Stop Soldier Suicide; Teri Embrey, Pritzker Military Museum and Library. My thanks go to the always helpful staff at New-York Historical Society and National Veterans Art Museum.

My readers: Annie Mitchell Smith, Theodore Knell, Kathy Pooler

My family, for their patience.

And to the men and women whose stories appear here – along with the friends they loved – and the many more whose stories are waiting to be told.

References:

Acton, Carol. *Grief in Wartime: Private Pain, Public Discourse*, New York, NY: Palgrave McMillan, 2007.

Baugh, Ben. "Veterans Form Bond to Cope with PTSD", stripes.com, March 9, 2014.

Bowden, Lisa and Shannon Cain, editors. *Powder: Writing by Women in the Ranks, from Vietnam to Iraq*, Tuscson, AZ: Kore Press, 2008.

Brock, Rita Nakashima and Rita Lettini, *Soul Repair: Recovering from Moral Injury After War*, Boston, MA: Beacon Press, 2012.

Brockett, Dr. L.P. *The Camp, The Battlefield, and The Hospital; or Lights and Shadows of the Great Rebellion*, Philadelphia, PA: National Publishing Co., 1866.

Childers, Thomas. *Soldier from the War Returning: The Greatest Generation's Troubled Homecoming from World War II*, New York, NY: Houghton Mifflin Harcourt, 2009.

Dokoupil, Tony. "A New Theory of PTSD and Veterans: Moral

Injury." *The Daily Beast*, Dec. 3, 2012.

Finkel, David. *Thank You For Your Service*, New York, NY: Farrar, Straus and Giroux, 2013.

Gould, Joe. "Drawing from Inspiration." Military Times, Sept. 20, 2013.

Hoge, MD, Charles W, Colonel, US Army (ret.). *Once A Warrior Always A Warrior.* Guiford, CT: GPP Life, 2010.

Holst-Warhaft, Gail. *The Cue for Passion: Grief and Its Political Uses*, Cambridge, MA: Harvard University Press, 2000.

Jadick, Cdr. Richard with Thomas Hayden. *On Call in Hell: A Doctor's Iraq War Story*, New York, NY: NAL Caliber, 2007.

Janis, Ted. "A Former Army Ranger Copes with His Friends Suicides and Asks What He Could Have Done to Help Them." *The Daily Beast*, Jan. 27, 2014.

Junger, Sebastian. *War*, New York, NY: Hatchette Book Group, 2011.

Kennedy, Kelly. *They Fought for Each Other*, New York, NY: St. Martin's Press, 2010.

Kipling, Rudyard. "Gunga Din", *Barrack Room Ballads*, 1892.

Knell, Theo. *A Hell for Heroes: A SAS Hero's Journey to the Heart of Darkness,* London: Hodder & Stoughton, 2012.

Martin, James A., Sparacino, Linette R., Belenky, Gregory, editors. *The Gulf War and Mental Health*, Westport, CT: Praeger Publishers, 1996.

Moore, Bret A. *Wheels Down: Adjusting to Life after Deployment*, Washington, DC: American Psychological Association, 2011.

Noakes, Vivien, editor. *Voices of Silence: The Alternative Book of*

1st World War Poetry, Phoenix Hill, UK: Sutton Publishing, Ltd., 2006.

Norman, Elizabeth. *Women at War: The Story of Fifty Military Nurses Who Served in Vietnam*, Philadelphia, PA: University of Pennsylvania Press, 1990.

Rubin, Allen, Weiss, Eugenia L., Coll, Jose E., editors. *Handbook of Military Social Work*, Hoboken, NJ: John Wiley & Sons, Inc., 2013.

Shakespeare, William. *Henry V*, Act IV, Scene iii

Skiba, Katherine M. *Sister in the Band of Brothers: Embedded with the 101st Airborne in Iraq*, Lawrence, KA: University Press of Kansas, 2005.

Trumbull, H. Clay. *War Memories of an Army Chaplain*, New York, NY: Charles Scribner's Sons, 1898.

"Veterans Day 2013: Nov. 11". US Census Bureau News, Washington, DC: US Dept. of Commerce, Oct. 31. 2013.

Whitfield, Donald H., editor. *Standing Down: From Warrior to Civilian*, Chicago, IL: The Great Books Foundation, 2013.

Wood, David. "Moral Injury: The Grunts – Damned If They Kill, Damned If They Don't", *The Huffington Post*. March 18, 2014.

Wood, David. "Moral Injury: The Recruits – When Right and Wrong Are Hard to Tell Apart", *The Huffington Post*. March 19, 2014

Wood, David. "Moral Injury: Healing – Can We Treat Moral Wounds?", *The Huffington Post*. March 20, 2014

Resources:

There are many organizations serving the needs of military men and women when they return home. Some are focused on physical and psychological challenges, others on basic needs such as jobs and housing. I've listed some here, because I've worked with and vetted them; I encourage you to support them. But please do your homework first, especially on their financials. There are a lot of scams out there, raising money in the name of wounded veterans. Only support those who deliver on their mission in a timely and cost-effective way.

Following are a few that assist active duty military and veterans to address PTSD, grief and other issues upon return to civilian life, as well as those that provide creative outlets. Additional resources can be found on my website. www.FriendGrief.com.

Military Outreach USA – www.militaryoutreachusa.org

Moral Injury – www.moralinjury.info

Stop Soldier Suicide – www.stopsoldiersuicide.org

Dryhootch – www.dryhootch.org

American Women Veterans – www.americanwomenveterans.org

National Veterans Art Museum – www.nvam.org

Make the Connection – www.maketheconnection.net

Journal of Military Experience – www.militaryexperience.org

Combat Stress (UK) – www.combatstress.org.uk

Military OneSource – www.militaryonesource.mil

Books by Victoria Noe

Friend Grief and Anger:
When Your Friend Dies and No One Gives A Damn

Friend Grief and AIDS:
Thirty Years of Burying Our Friends

Friend Grief and 9/11:
The Forgotten Mourners

Friend Grief and the Military:
Band of Friends

Coming:

Friend Grief in the Workplace:
More Than An Empty Cubicle

Victoria Noe has been a writer most of her life, but didn't admit it until 2009. After earning a masters degree in Speech and Dramatic Art from the University of Iowa, she moved to Chicago, where she worked professionally as a stage manager, director and administrator in addition to being a founding board member of the League of Chicago Theatres. She then transferred her skills to being a professional fundraiser, raising money for arts, educational and AIDS service organizations, and later an award-winning sales consultant of children's books. Noe also trained hundreds of people around the country in marketing, event planning and grant writing. But after a concussion impacted her ability to continue in sales, she switched gears to keep a promise to a dying friend to write a book.

That book is now an award-winning series. The first three – *Friend Grief and Anger: When Your Friend Dies and No One Gives A Damn; Friend Grief and AIDS: Thirty Years of*

Burying Our Friends and *Friend Grief and 9/11: The Forgotten Mourners* were published in 2013. Following *Friend Grief and the Military: Band of Friends* will be *Friend Grief in the Workplace: More Than an Empty Cubicle*, in the fall of 2014.

Noe is a member of Alliance of Independent Authors (ALLI), Chicago Writers Association, Military Writers Society of America and ACT UP/NY. Her freelance articles have appeared on numerous grief and writing blogs as well as *Windy City Times*, *Chicago Tribune* and *Huffington Post*. In addition, she feeds her reading habit by reviewing a wide variety of books on BroadwayWorld.com. A native St. Louisan, she's a lifelong Cardinals fan and will gladly take on any comers in musical theatre trivia. Her website, www.FriendGrief.com, was named one of the top ten grief support websites in 2012. You can follow her on Twitter @ Victoria_Noe.

www.ingramcontent.com/pod-product-compliance
Lightning Source LLC
Chambersburg PA
CBHW070927010526
44110CB00056B/2263